LEVEL 1

Maria's Dilemma

Julia Newsome

Richmond READERS

Richmond READERS

LEVEL 1

(500 headwords)

Maria's Dilemma

Oscar

Jack's Game

The Boy from Yesterday

The Black Mountain

LEVEL 2

(800 headwords)

Jason Causes Chaos

Craigen Castle Mystery

The Road through the Hills and othes stories

Where's Mauriac?

Saturday Storm

LEVEL 3

(1200 headwords)

A Trip to the Stars

Dr Jekyll and Mr Hyde

The Canterville Ghost and Other Stories

Cold Feet

Frankenstein

LEVEL 4

(1800 headwords)

A Trip to London

Dracula

Jane Eyre

The Adventures of Tom Sawyer

Sense and Sensibility

LEVEL 5

(2600+ headwords)

Steve Jobs: the man behind Apple

Elizabeth II The Diamond Queen

Maria's Dilemma

Maria's Dilemma is the story of a young student from southern Europe. She is studying at university in the north of England. But things are going badly and she cannot continue her studies. Suddenly, early one morning, she sees the answer to her problems and she enters into a world of mystery and crime...

....

Julia Newsome taught English to people at work and children at school for twenty years in Athens, Greece. She now lives half the time in Belgium and the other half in England, but she often visits Greece. She teaches English and writes stories and teaching books. She likes going to the cinema and walking in the country. Julia has two children.

LEVEL 1

CHARACTERS IN THE STORY

Melvin Beecham, a rich businessman, married to Harriet

Maria Adami, a student from southern Europe

Barry Lyle, Lisa's new husband

Yuri, a student in Maria's department at university

Bill and Maggie, police detectives

young man with black bag, works for Barry Lyle

Detective Chief Inspector Wheeler

Lisa Stroud-Lyle, Harriet's younger sister

Mr Sakks, Barry Lyle's business partner

── CHAPTER 1 ──
By the River

Maria could* not sleep. She put on her clothes and her coat and went out. She walked along by the river. It was early morning and the sun came up slowly. She had a letter from her father in her hand. There was no more money for her studies.

The river was quiet here. She looked at the sky and the trees in the water. She walked under the trees and thought* about her problems. Far away in southern Europe her father was ill and could not work.

There was no more money for her studies.

Then her foot hit something on the ground. It was a shoe. Maria looked at the water. The river moved very slowly here and the sun on the water was very strong. Maria closed her eyes. Then she looked again. There was a foot in the shoe. Then she saw the face, a woman's face, under the water. The woman was very white. She wore* a green dress and a beautiful green necklace. She was dead.

Maria screamed*. She called for help. No one came. She looked at the woman. She looked at the necklace. She began* to feel calmer.

'That necklace is the answer to my problems,' Maria thought. 'I can sell it. I can pay for my studies with the money. No! What am I thinking? I can't. I can't take things from a dead woman.' Maria did not move. 'But no one is going to know...'

■ ■ ■

She put her hands in the water. It was cold. The dead woman was cold, too. She quickly took the necklace and put it in her bag. No one saw her.

She moved away and the dead woman moved in the water.

'What am I doing?' she thought. She began to cry. She ran* away from the river. She wanted to be in her room in the university again. She didn't want to see anyone. She didn't want to tell anyone.

'Hey, Maria! What's the matter? Hey, stop...' Yuri, a friend from her class, stopped her. He saw her crying

Maria quickly took the necklace and put it in her bag.

and he wanted to help. 'What's the matter, Maria?'

'I s–saw a d–dead w–woman in the river,' Maria said.
'I feel ... oh, Yuri, I am so c–cold ... She was v–very
white...'

'It's OK. It's all right.' Yuri went with Maria to
telephone the police. Then they went to Yuri's room
and waited. Yuri made them some tea.

Ten minutes later, the police came and asked Maria
about what happened. She told* them and they all went
to the river. The police did not ask her about the
necklace.

Maria went to her room. She took the necklace out
of her bag and put it between her clean clothes.

'So now I am rich,' she thought, and she was happy. 'Now I can finish my studies.' She began to write a letter to her father.

But later she thought, 'No, I am not rich. I can't sell that necklace. What I did was wrong.' She wasn't happy. She stopped writing the letter.

■ ■ ■

She thought and thought about it all night. Again Maria could not sleep.

Maria put the necklace between her clean clothes.

The next day, Maria got a newspaper. She took it to her room. There was a photograph of the dead woman. She was with her husband in front of a castle. Her name was Harriet Beecham and she was rich and beautiful.

Woman Dies In River

Harriet Beecham with her husband, Melvin, last summer in front of their home, Hadburgh Castle

Mrs Harriet Beecham, 35, of Hadburgh Castle, died on Saturday evening. She fell* into the River Had and hit her head. She died at once. Maria Adami, an Italian student, found* Mrs Beecham on Sunday morning. The dead woman was five kilometres down the river, near the university.

On Saturday, Mrs Beecham's sister, Lisa Stroud, married* Barry Lyle of Manchester. There was a big party at the castle on Saturday night.

No one knows what time Mrs Beecham left* the party. The police think she was afraid of something. They say she ran down to the river. She lost* one of her shoes.

The dead woman's husband, Melvin Beecham, is asking for information.

'Maybe someone from the village saw something,' he said. 'I don't understand it. Harriet was very happy at the party. She talked to everyone and danced a lot. I know that something terrible happened. Please help the police to find the answer.'

Maria finished reading. She took the necklace from between her clothes. It was very beautiful.

'I must sell it,' she thought. 'Who can I sell it to?' She opened the newspaper again. Was there a shop in London where she could sell it? Maybe at the back of the newspaper...

She looked up. Someone was at the door!

Maria left the newspaper on the sofa and put the necklace between her clothes again. She felt hot and ill. She opened the door.

——— C H A P T E R **3** ———

A Visit from the Police

A tall, dark man and a shorter, dark woman were at the door.

'Maria Adami?' the man asked.

'Yes.'

'We are police detectives,' the woman said. 'I am Maggie and this is Bill. Can we come in?'

'Yes,' Maria said. They came in. Bill saw the newspaper.

'You're famous,' he said.

Maria couldn't speak. Her face was white.

'Sit down, Maria,' Maggie said. 'I must ask you some questions.' They all sat* down. 'Now. What time did you find Mrs Beecham?' she asked.

'We are police detectives,' the woman said. 'Can we come in?'

'About seven thirty in the morning,' Maria answered.

'Did you see what clothes she had on?'

Maria knew* what to say. 'I saw a shoe – only one shoe. And a green dress. I saw white arms – and a lot of long, dark hair.'

'Did you see a necklace, an emerald necklace?'

'I didn't see anything more. I was afraid. I ran away.'

'Yes, of course.'

'Harriet Beecham's husband wants to know about the necklace,' Bill explained. 'He thinks it is important. It was very expensive. Maybe someone killed Mrs Beecham because they wanted it.'

'I – I don't know. I didn't see it.' Maria waited. She felt ill.

'OK, Maria, thank you,' Maggie said. She stood up. 'So we can tell Mr Beecham there was no necklace when you found her.' She looked at Maria for some moments.

Maria looked at Maggie.

'That's right,' she said.

'If you remember anything more, please telephone us.' Bill gave Maria the number.

'Yes, of course,' she said quietly.

'Goodbye, Maria.'

They left. Maria closed the door.

'What am I doing?' she thought, 'I take a necklace from a dead person. I tell a lie* to the police. What am I going to do...?

'I'm going to take this very expensive necklace to

Bill gave Maria the telephone number of the local police station.

London. I'm going to find someone to buy it. I'm going to put the money in the bank. I'm going to finish my studies. I'm going to go home to my family and get a very good job. That's what I'm going to do. It isn't going to be easy, but I must do it.'

It was eleven o'clock. Maria had a class. She took her books and went out.

A man got out of a car and walked behind her.

In the windows Maria saw a man following her.

Chapter 4

Partners

Maria heard* someone behind her. She walked along near some big windows. In the windows she saw a man following her. She stopped. He stopped and looked at a newspaper. She went on. He followed her again. She felt afraid, but she wanted to laugh, too. She moved, he moved. She stopped, he stopped.

Maria looked at the man. She said, 'Are you following me? I'm going to class. Do you want to come too?'

He was very surprised and he laughed.

'Who are you?' Maria asked.

'Er ... I...' He did not want to tell her.

Maria began to walk away. She was late for class. He ran in front of her.

'I'm Barry Lyle. Harriet Beecham is – was – my wife's sister.'

Maria went cold. What did he want from her? She looked at his face. 'I'm sorry about Harriet,' she said.

'Oh. Harriet ... Yes. Thank you,' he said. 'You didn't know Harriet?'

'No, I didn't know her,' Maria said.

'Ah ... What happened after you found her?' Barry asked.

'The police took her away. I didn't watch.'

'I see. Did they look for her ... er ... shoe there, where you found her?'

'I don't know. I didn't stay.'

'Are the police there now? Can we go and see?'

Maria thought, 'I'm never going there again.' Her face was white and her eyes were hard. She looked at him and said, 'I'm sorry. I can't. I must go to my class.'

'I'm sorry. It was horrible for you.' Barry talked quickly and quietly. 'I want to help her husband, Melvin, you see. He's very sad, you know, and doesn't want to see anyone or leave the house.'

Barry smiled at her. Then he gave her a piece of paper.

Maria *thought*, 'Is that true?' but she *said*, 'I can't help. I don't remember any more. The police asked me this morning. Why don't you talk to them?'

'This is family business, you see,' he said. And he smiled at her. It was a beautiful smile. For a moment she felt* he was her friend, her special friend.

'If you remember anything – or find anything – tell me,' he said. He gave her a piece of paper. 'Here's the telephone number at the castle. I live there now I am married to Lisa. Call me before you tell the police, OK?'

'Oh, yes ... er ... I ... OK.' Maria looked at him again. His eyes were sky blue.

'Call me any time,' he said. 'Not Melvin or the police. You understand me, don't you?'

Maria was afraid. Did he know that she had the necklace? Maybe, maybe not.

'Yes, I understand,' she said. She smiled, too. 'No one except you.'

'That's right,' he said. 'Partners.'

'Now I must go,' she said. He began to go with her. She laughed and said, 'You don't need to follow me now. We're partners.'

He laughed, too. 'No, I don't. I followed the police to where you live and I know where you go to class. I can find you any time.' He took her hand and looked at her. He smiled, but his eyes were cold now. 'Have a good class. See you later.'

'Bye,' Maria said, and went through the doors.

—— CHAPTER **5** ——

The Young Man with the Black Bag

After class Maria and Yuri stopped at the Campus Café for a sandwich. She told Yuri about Barry, but not about the necklace.

'You must tell the police,' he said.

'Maybe ... if he follows me again,' she answered.

They had coffee and Maria saw a young man with a big, black bag and a mobile phone looking at her. 'I'm afraid of everyone, now,' she thought. 'I'm imagining things.'

Later she and Yuri walked home. She said goodbye to Yuri at her door. In the little park across the road she saw the young man with the black bag. He sat reading a newspaper. He had a drink and a sandwich.

Maria went up to her room. She looked at the emerald necklace. 'I can go to London tomorrow. Today I must prepare,' she thought. 'But people are following me and I'm afraid. This is wrong. I must give the necklace to the police... Yes, but then where can I find the money to continue my studies? I can't work *and* study. I must sell the necklace.' She opened the newspaper again. 'What am I going to do?'

In the little park across the road she saw the young man with the black bag and a mobile phone.

─── CHAPTER **6** ───
At the Castle

At the castle, Lisa, Barry's wife, waited. When she heard his car, she went to the door. Her face was red from crying.

'Is everything OK?' she asked Barry.

'I think so,' he answered. 'I saw the police this morning. They asked me a lot of questions about Harriet and her shoe and her emeralds.'

'They were our mother's emeralds. The necklace was so beautiful...' She began crying again.

'Did Harriet have a safe* in the house?' Barry asked.

'What do you mean?'

'A safe where she put her expensive things and important papers. Maybe the necklace is there.'

'I don't think so,' Lisa said. She put her hand on Barry's arm. 'It's so horrible. Poor, poor Harriet...'

Barry moved away. 'Yes, yes. You go back to bed. Dr Madsen is coming soon. I must telephone someone.'

Lisa went up to her room. She could not stop crying. Barry was always too busy and she felt so sad.

■ ■ ■

Barry called a number.

'Is Mr Sakks there?' he said.

'Who is this, please?' someone answered.

'Barry Lyle.'

'Yes, Mr Lyle. Just a moment...'

'Sakks here.'

Lisa put her hand on Barry's arm. 'It's so horrible. Poor, poor Harriet...'

'The stuff is excellent this time. It's selling very well,' Sakks
said. 'No police, lots of money. I like that.'

'I think we have a problem,' Barry said.

'*I* don't have any problems,' Sakks answered. 'The stuff * is excellent this time. It's selling very well. No police, lots of money. I like that. Maybe *you* have a problem, but *I* don't.' Barry heard Sakks laugh.

'Did you read about Harriet Beecham?'

'Yeah•, little Lisa's sister. She died.'

'At the party on Saturday night she told me she knew about my business with you,' Barry said. Sakks did not speak. 'She said, "I have a recording on a USB drive of you two on the phone. I know about Sakks and the drugs. I couldn't stop you marrying Lisa. But I can stop you and Sakks selling drugs to children."'

Sakks was quiet for a moment.

'Did *you* kill her?' he asked.

'No, I didn't kill her. She was afraid of me and ran away.'

'Why?'

'I told her I knew about her past. I said, "When you were young, you took drugs and the police caught* you." I said to her, "I'm going to tell Melvin about it. He thinks drugs are the worst thing you can do." She ran out of the house. I don't know how she fell in the river. Yesterday morning that student found her, dead.'

'So what's the problem? She can't talk now.'

'Where is the USB drive?' Barry answered.

'I don't think there is a USB drive,' Sakks said.

•*Colloquial form of* Yes

'I know about your past,' Barry said to Harriet. 'I'm going to tell Melvin about it.'

'Oh, there is. It wasn't a lie.'

'Then you must find it. Ask her husband where she put important things. Ask your wife.'

'I did,' Barry answered. 'Lisa doesn't know. I have someone watching the Adami girl, too.'

'Good. Ask Harriet's husband about her bank. Maybe she had a safety deposit box* there. I can get the number if I know which bank.'

'OK.'

'Call me later,' Sakks said. 'Today!'

'Of course,' Barry answered.

─── C H A P T E R **7** ───

Barry looks for the USB Drive

⑧

Dr Madsen came and Barry took her up to see Lisa. When he came down, Melvin was at the door.

'Hello, Barry. How is Lisa?' Melvin asked.

'She never stops crying. Dr Madsen is with her now.'

'I want to cry all the time, too. But ... men don't cry, do they?' Melvin said. 'I couldn't work today, so I came home.'

'You loved Harriet a lot, didn't you?' Barry said.

'I love Harriet now. Maybe more. She is – was – a very good person. She helped people with their problems – drug problems and other problems. And she loved me. I ... I ... don't think I knew how much.' There were tears* in Melvin's eyes.

'And she loved me,' Melvin said. 'I ... I ... don't think I knew how much.'

'Do you think that Harriet's necklace is in the house?' Barry asked. 'Or maybe at the bank? Did she have a safe somewhere?'

'I can't think now, Barry. I'm sorry. I must go to my room.'

■ ■ ■

Barry went to Harriet's study*. He wanted to know the name of her bank. But he couldn't find anything about it. Barry didn't know what to do next.

Chapter 8

Maria Decides what to Do

Maria didn't know what to do next. She sat on her sofa, thinking. She sat there all afternoon. She cried. She got angry. She cried again.

'What am I going to do?' She was very tired and she went to sleep.

When she got up it was evening. She knew what to do. She must tell Mr Beecham that she found the necklace by the river. She must tell him she wanted a lot of money and that he must give it to her. No money, no necklace.

Maria didn't know what to do next.

She telephoned the castle and asked for Mr Beecham.

'Can we meet?' she said. 'I need to talk to you.' He agreed to meet her at the Campus Café.

■ ■ ■

It was dark. The young man with the black bag sat at a table by the window. Melvin and Maria sat by the wall.

'What do you want to talk about?' Melvin asked. He thought, 'She is very white. She looks ill.' He said, 'Are you OK?'

She looked at him and he smiled. He had a friendly face but his eyes were sad. Maria thought, 'Now I must be strong.' She began to speak.

'Mr Beecham, I have something of Harriet's,' she said. 'If you want it, you must ... I ... I...' She could not continue.

'What? What have you got?' Melvin asked. He put his hand on her arm. 'Please tell me.'

Maria began to cry. She cried quietly, her head down. Melvin waited. The young man with the black bag watched them.

Maria began to talk. Melvin could not hear her at first.

'...because I wanted to put the money in the bank. Then I can stay here next year. I can continue with my studies. But I can't ask you for money for Harriet's necklace. I thought I could, but I can't. They are your emeralds. I can't sell you *your* emeralds.' She looked up at him. 'I'm so sorry.'

Melvin thought a moment. 'You're afraid about next

year and you're very young,' he said, 'but you're not bad. It's all right. Don't cry any more ... Can you give me the necklace now?'

'Yes, yes. It's in my room. It's not far.'

■ ■ ■

They left the café. The young man with the black bag followed them.

In her room, Maria gave Melvin the necklace. He sat down on the sofa and looked and looked at it. Maria waited.

'She wore this the day I married her,' he said.

Maria sat next to him. 'I'm very sorry. I did a very bad thing and I'm very sorry.'

Melvin opened the largest emerald in the necklace. Maria watched in surprise. It was a very small box, and in it there was a piece of paper and a key.

'Where is my hair?' he asked. 'She had some of my hair in here.' He was surprised. 'Why did she take it out?' He looked at the key.

'Ah,' Maria said, 'now I think I understand... Mr Beecham, look through the window. Do you see that young man in the park?'

'What...? Where...? Yes, I see him. The man with the mobile phone. Who is he?'

'He follows me everywhere. He was in the café. He is a friend of Barry Lyle's,' Maria explained.

It was a very small box, and in it there was a piece of paper and a key.

'Barry? Lisa's husband?' Melvin did not understand.

'Yes. Barry thinks I have something of Harriet's – something he wants,' said Maria. 'I thought it was the emeralds, but now I think it is this piece of paper. What is the number on it?'

'It's the number and the key of her safety deposit box at the bank ... I remember now. Barry asked me about a safe this afternoon. He wants this key. But why...? I must go to the police!'

'The police?' Maria did not want to see those detectives again. 'I can't come with you. I'm sorry.'

Melvin smiled. 'It's OK. I don't need you with me. I can say I found the emeralds somewhere at home.'

'Yes, I... You are a very good man, Mr Beecham. Thank you.' Maria felt better.

■ ■ ■

Melvin left Maria and went to the police station. The young man with the black bag and the mobile phone followed him.

—— CHAPTER **9** ——

A Good Night's Sleep

Melvin explained everything to the police. The inspector telephoned the bank manager* and Melvin met* him at the bank. The bank manager opened the doors and gave the safety deposit box to Melvin.

Melvin opened the box. There was a USB drive and a letter in it. Part of the letter said:

> Barry Lyle is working with Sakks.
> They are selling drugs to children.

Harriet's name was at the bottom.

Melvin thanked the bank manager and went back to the police station. The young man with the black bag did not follow him. He was with Barry and Sakks at the castle. They took all Barry's things and got into a big car. They left Lisa sleeping and drove* away.

At the police station the inspector and a policeman got into a police car. They followed Melvin to the castle. When they got there, they found only Lisa.

■ ■ ■

Maria wanted to talk to someone. She walked to Yuri's. No one followed her. She told Yuri everything. When she finished, he did not say she was bad or wrong.

'So what are you going to do next year?' he asked.

'I don't know,' she answered. 'I only know I must study hard now. Maybe my father can begin working again. Or maybe I can get a job in the evenings. Maybe the university can help me again.'

'If they see you are studying hard, maybe they can,' Yuri said.

Maria smiled. 'I'm going home. I'm so tired. Thank

They got into a big car and drove away.

you for listening.'

'We can meet for lunch tomorrow, if you want,' Yuri said. 'We can go to the cinema in the evening.'

'Thank you, Yuri. That's a good idea.'

■ ■ ■

Next morning Maria woke up at ten o'clock. She smiled. It was good to sleep well again.

11

———— CHAPTER 10 ————

An Invitation to the Castle

Four weeks later Maria got an invitation.

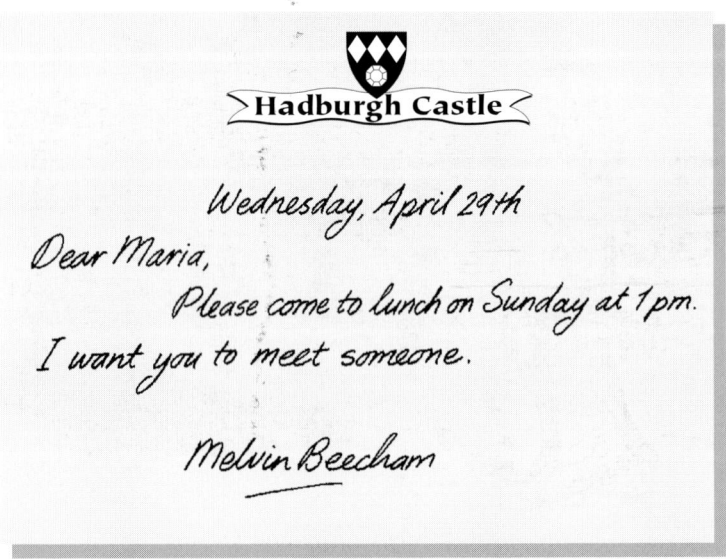

Hadburgh Castle

Wednesday, April 29th

Dear Maria,
        Please come to lunch on Sunday at 1pm.
I want you to meet someone.

Melvin Beecham

Yuri laughed when he saw it. 'Lunch at the castle. Wow! You are important.'

'I don't think I am,' Maria said. 'I feel very bad about what I did. I must go, of course, but I don't want to.'

■ ■ ■

On Sunday it rained. Maria took a bus to Hadburgh village and walked slowly up to the castle. She felt sad and nervous. The castle was big and dark.

Maria felt sad and nervous. The castle was big and dark.

A young woman opened the door.

'Are you Maria Adami?' she said. 'Hello, I'm Lisa Lyle. Come in.'

The rain stopped. Lisa took Maria into the dining room*. Sun filled the room. Through the big windows Maria could see the river. There were yellow flowers on the table.

Melvin took Maria's hand. There was a man with grey hair with him.

'This is Detective Chief Inspector* Wheeler,' Melvin said. 'Maria Adami.'

'Nice to meet you,' the policeman said.

Maria looked at Melvin. He did not smile. She looked at Inspector Wheeler.

'Nice to meet you, too,' she said.

They sat down at the table. Maria could not eat.

'We know now that Mrs Beecham – Harriet – fell into the river by accident,' Inspector Wheeler said. 'We have Barry Lyle and Mr Sakks at the police station now. We caught them on Friday, thanks to you and Mr Beecham.'

'That's great,' Maria said.

'I need you to tell the court* what happened. You can explain how you found Mrs Beecham and that Barry Lyle followed you,' the Chief Inspector said. 'Are you going to be here in the summer?'

'Oh … I don't know.' Maria looked at Melvin. Melvin slowly ate a piece of meat. 'I don't know if I can stay,' Maria said. 'I have no more money.'

Now Melvin looked at Maria and said, 'I talked to your university last week ... They say you are doing very well.' He smiled. 'So I am going to put some money into your bank every month. Then you can finish your studies.'

Maria didn't know what to say. She wanted to dance. She stood up and walked round the table to Melvin.

'Thank you, Mr Beecham,' she said and gave him a kiss. He took her hand and laughed.

'Work hard,' he said.

'Thank you, Mr Beecham,' she said and gave him a kiss.

By the River Again

The next morning Maria got up early. She walked along by the river. The sun on the water was very strong. Maria closed her eyes.

'Poor Harriet,' she thought. 'You are dead and I am alive. And, thanks to you and Mr Beecham, I am so happy.' She looked up and saw Yuri. He walked up to her and looked into her face.

'Why did you come here?' he said. 'You said you never wanted to come here again.'

Maria smiled.

'I wanted to say goodbye to Harriet – and to thank her.'

■ ■ ■

Yuri and Maria walked along by the river, hand in hand.

Yuri and Maria walked along by the river, hand in hand.

E X E R C I S E S

▨ Comprehension

Chapter 1 By the River
1 What are Maria's problems as the story begins?
2 What is in the river?
3 What does Maria take?
4 What does Maria want to do with it?

Chapter 2 In the News
1 What is the dead woman's name?
2 Where did she live?
3 How did she die?
4 When did she die?

Chapter 3 A Visit from the Police
1 Who are Maggie and Bill?
2 What does Maggie want to know?
3 What does Maria tell her about the necklace?
4 Is what Maria says true?
5 Why does Maria go out at eleven o'clock?

Chapter 4 Partners
1 Why does Maria want to laugh?
2 Who is following Maria?
3 What does he want Maria to do?
4 Does he need to follow her after he talks to her?
5 Why/Why not?

Chapter 5 The Young Man with the Black Bag
1 Who do you think the young man with the black bag is?
2 Is Maria happy about selling the necklace?
3 Why/Why not?

Chapter 6 At the Castle
1 Who is Lisa?
2 When did Lisa and Barry marry? (see Chapter 2)

3 How does Lisa feel?
4 What did Harriet know about Barry and Sakks?
5 What does Barry know about Harriet?
6 Did Barry kill Harriet?
7 What does Barry want to find?
8 Where does Sakks think they are?

Chapter 7 Barry looks for the USB Drive

1 What problems did Harriet help people with?
2 Why does Melvin want to go to his room?
3 Where does Barry look for information about Harriet's bank?

Chapter 8 Maria Decides what to Do

1 Who does Maria decide to sell the necklace to?
2 How did Maria know Mr Beecham's telephone number?
3 Maria and Melvin meet in the Campus Café. Another person is there. Who?
4 Why does Maria begin to cry?
5 What does Melvin do with the necklace?
6 What does he find in it?
7 Is Melvin going to tell the police that Maria took the necklace?

Chapter 9 A Good Night's Sleep

1 What does Melvin find in the safety deposit box?
2 How does Barry know that Melvin is with the police?
3 Who does Maria tell everything to?
4 What does he invite her to do?
5 Why does Maria sleep well?

Chapter 10 An Invitation to the Castle

1 Does Maria want to go to the castle for lunch?
2 Did Melvin tell anyone that Maria took the necklace?
3 Do the police think that Harriet Beecham was killed by someone?
4 What does Melvin say he is going to do every month?
5 How does Maria feel when he tells her?
6 What does she do?

Chapter 11 By the River Again

1 What is the last chapter of the story similar to?
2 Why does Maria go to the river again?

B Working with Language

1 **Imagine Maria is talking to the court. Write what she says in the past tense.**

'I am by the river. I have a problem and I want to be quiet and think. The sun on the water is strong. I cannot see. My foot hits something. It is in the water. I see a shoe. I close my eyes and then look again. I see a shoe and there is a foot in it. Then I see a white face. It is a woman. She has a lot of hair. She is wearing a green dress. I scream and I call. No one comes. I cannot see anyone. The woman is dead. She does not move.'

2 **Use these prepositions to complete the sentences below.**

from   next to   between   into   under   through
at   up   by   in front of

1 There was a woman's face ... the water.
2 Maria put the necklace ... her clean clothes.
3 Harriet Beecham was with her husband ... a castle.
4 What did Barry want ... her?
5 'Here's the telephone number ... the castle,' Barry said.
6 'Bye,' Maria said and she went ... the doors.
7 Maria said goodbye at her door and went ... to her room.
8 Maria and Melvin sat ... the wall.
9 Maria sat ... Melvin on the sofa. 'I'm very sorry,' she said.
10 They took all Barry's things and got ... a big car.

C Activities

1 Write a letter. Choose a or b.

a You are Maria. Yesterday, you told Yuri everything. You are writing to a close friend back at home. Do you want to tell him/her everything?

b You are Yuri. Yesterday, Maria told you everything. Write to your brother and tell him about your studies and about Maria. Tell him how you feel about her.

2 Write a short dialogue.

It is the day after Maria's lunch at the castle. She telephones her father with the good news. Imagine their conversation.

GLOSSARY

bank manager *(n)* the most important person in a bank

began *(v)* past tense of *begin*

caught *(v)* past tense of *catch*

could *(v)* past tense of *can*

court *(n)* a tribunal

Detective Chief Inspector *(n)* the most important police officer in the region

dining room *(n)* the room where you eat

drove *(v)* past tense of *drive*

fell *(v)* past tense of *fall*

felt *(v)* past tense of *feel*

found *(v)* past tense of *find*

heard *(v)* past tense of *hear*

knew *(v)* past tense of *know*

left *(v)* past tense of *leave*

lie *(n)* something that is not true

lost *(v)* past tense of *lose*

marry *(v)* when a man and woman *marry*, they are husband and wife

met *(v)* past tense of *meet*

ran *(v)* past tense of *run*

safe *(n)* a strong box (sometimes in the wall behind a picture) where you put important things; no one can open it without the number

safety deposit box *(n)* a strong box in a bank where you put important things and only you have the key

sat *(v)* past tense of *sit*

scream *(v)* Maria *screams* because she is afraid

study *(n)* a room used for reading, writing and studying

stuff *(n)* things; here it means drugs

tears *(n)* usually *plural*; when you cry, *tears* come out of your eyes

thought *(v)* past tense of *think*

told *(v)* past tense of *tell*

wore *(v)* past tense of *wear*

◪ Richmond

58 St Aldates
Oxford
OX1 1ST
United Kingdom

Publishing Director: Sarah Thorpe
Managing Editor: Tanya Whatling
Editor: Jane Holt

Cover Illustration: David Axtell
Illustrations: Pat Ludlow, Gema Arquero
Recording: Maria Jeanette Christiansen, Mauri Corretjé

Printed in Spain
ISBN: 978-84-668-1555-0

© Richmond / Santillana Educación S.L., 2012